Brandon Hurst

Nadezda Solovieva

First published in Great Britain in 2006
by Beyond Black
Beyond Black is an imprint of A Jot
26 Thurloe Street
London SW7 2LT
UK

ISBN 1-905904-10-X
978-1-905904-10-5
Design: Maxim Lachmann
Illustration: Nadia Solovieva
Editor: Ned Ahajot

Printed and bound in Poland by
Bialostockie Zaklady Graficzne SA
Al. Tysiaclecia P. Polskiego 2
15-111 Bialystok

Brandon Hurst
Nadezda Solovieva

beyond black

£
£
JIMMY

Contents

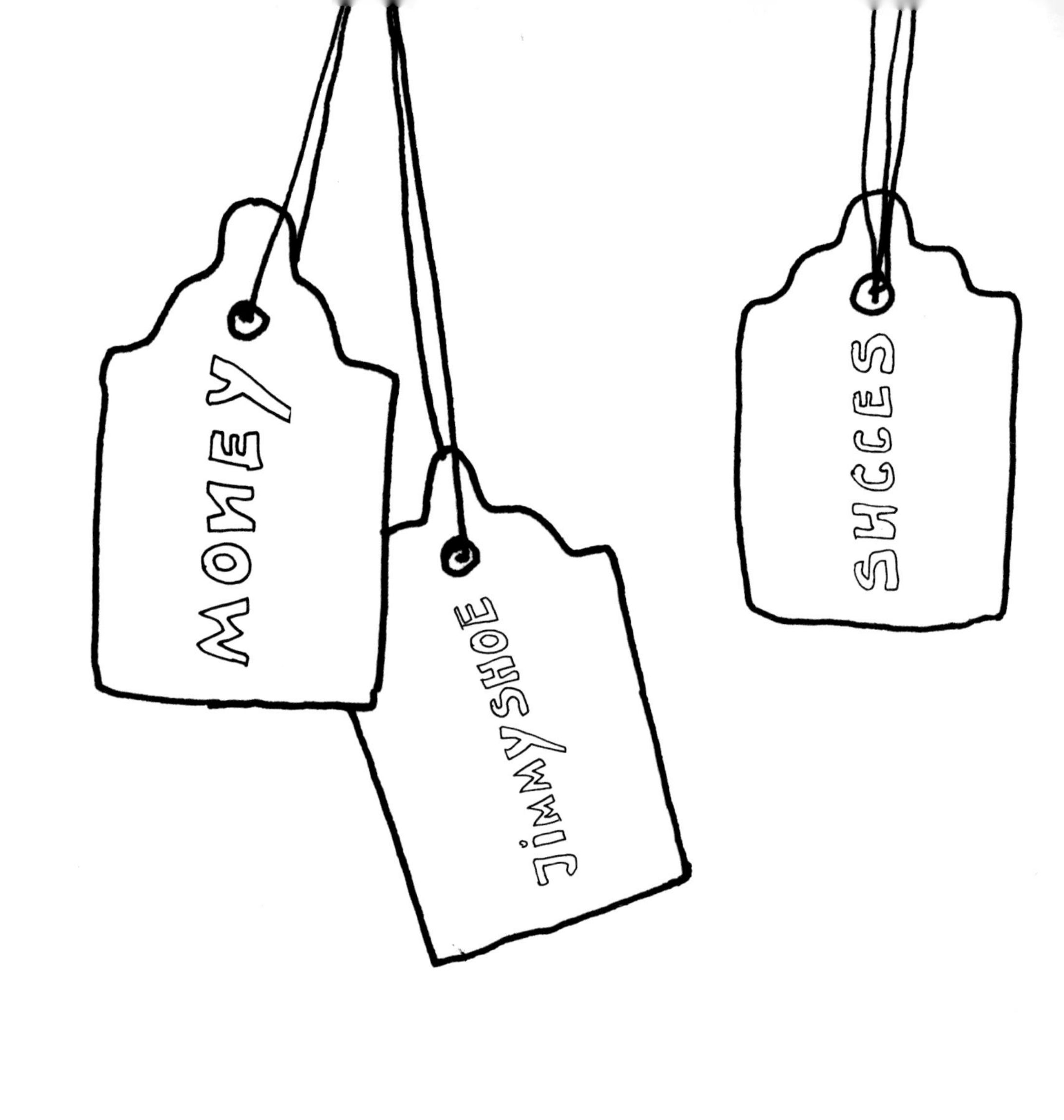
MONEY
JIMMYSHOE
SUCCES

CHAPTER 1

Hackney Basement to Hollywood Belles

The Choo shoe is one that every woman wants to wear because it makes her foot look irresistible and says something exciting, inspiring and impressive about her taste and wealth.

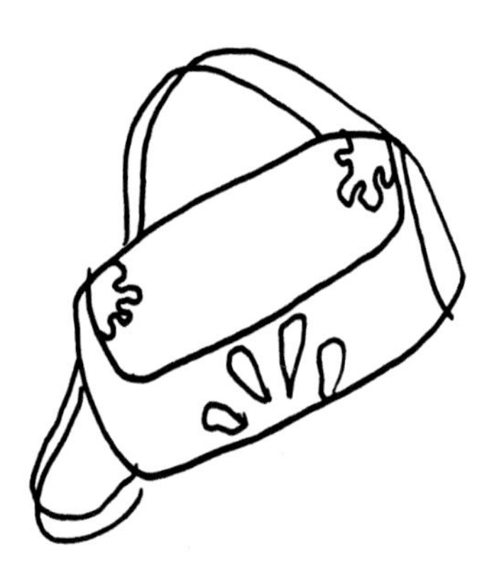

As little as ten years ago, when Malaysian cobbler Jimmy Choo was making and selling just a few pairs of shoes a week out of his basement workshop in one of London's less well-regarded neighbourhoods, he could hardly have imagined that his name would become the label of an international footwear sensation. From his origins a decade ago in a dilapidated old hospital building, he has founded and inspired a phenomenon that is celebrated in fashion magazines and on catwalks the world over. Even the phrase 'Jimmy Choos' has passed into the vernacular as a synonym for a pair of shoes – a piece of rhyming slang only made possible by the fact that the registrar misspelt his real name, Chow, on his birth certificate.

Whilst Jimmy's 'dainty and deadly' stilettos were for years beloved amongst a highly select list of clients that included Diana, Princess of Wales, it took the money, talent and the glamour of Tamara Mellon to take his sexy, stylish creations global. For the next ten years, her pushy marketing was to haul the company out of its Hackney basement and onto the feet of royalty, celebrities and socialites the world over.

Along the way there were casualties: she had to deal with the break-up of her marriage, a highly publicised affair with a kiss'n'tell toyboy, and a bust-up with her co-founder, Jimmy himself. But **whatever** her own losses, the company she launched – now rivalled only by Manolo **Blahnik** – has never done anything short of win.

CHAPTER 2

Mr Jimmy Choo

Jimmy Choo is a Hakka Chinese who was born in Penang, Malaysia. He hails from a family of shoemakers, and it is the stuff of legend in the trade that he cobbled his first pair at the tender age of 11. Although he has now far surpassed the fame and skill of his parents, he credits them with instilling in him the healthy reverence for footwear that has lasted his whole life. His father, Kee Yin, was a well-regarded craftsman of men and women's moccasins in Penang. 'I have always loved shoes. I used to love to watch my father make shoes and see how people respected him for his skill,' Jimmy told *Footwear News*. From his childhood, when he learned about the craft in his father's factory, he had a strong awareness that making shoes was not merely about covering the feet.

'My father was not just making shoes,' he maintains. 'He was creating something to do with his heart and his mind, and transferring it to the human feet. He told me that it was not just about making shoes and money. It was about being an artist. There is no point if it is not art.'

Jimmy started making shoes in the 1970s. 'I studied at Shih Chung primary school up to Year Six and after that, I had to help my late father, Choo Kee Yin, at his shop where I learnt shoe-making skills,' he said. His father took a personal hand in training him at the family craft. 'Patience is everything if you want to learn, my old man used to say.' In 1980, when he was 19, Jimmy travelled to England to further his education at Cordwainers Technical College in Hackney, which provided a unique opportunity to study footwear, saddlery and leathercraft. Cordwainers has since been incorporated into the prestigious London College of Fashion. '

My father paid for the college fees for the first year but for the remaining three years, I had to work part-time in restaurants and a shoe factory to pay for the fees and my living costs,' he said. His work at the factory included menial tasks such as cleaning the toilets and sweeping the floor. It was his intention to finish his diploma and then head back to his parents in Malaysia.

The early 80s saw an upsurge in the field of British shoe design, and Jimmy studied alongside some of the leaders of this blossoming talent – Emma Hope, Patrick Cox and others. His English, still rather faltering now, was much worse in those days, cause for amusement among the students and staff at Cordwainers. 'I was worse before,' he told *New Straights Times* in 2005.

Jimmy would warn his vsiting up-market clients: 'This is not a very nice place.'

What they couldn't laugh at was his obvious talent, and Jimmy remembers with glee a recent chance meeting with one of his professors who had always been entertained by his poor English. Now that he was a world-renowned designer, the shoe was on the other foot. 'The thing is never to stop learning' is one of the secrets that he gives for his success.

When he graduated – with distinction, naturally – from his studies, Jimmy made good his intention and returned to Malaysia. But working for his father just wasn't the same. 'I went home for a year, but I had gotten used to the life here and came back,' he remembers. Perhaps that was true, but perhaps he also recognised the opportunities that lay open to him in England. On his return, he got a job working as a shoe design consultant for Bally of Switzerland. Within a couple of years, Jimmy had gained enough experience to step out and start his own line. Compared to the luxury boutiques that now bear his name, his beginnings were modest.

In 1986, Jimmy hired a few rooms to use as a workshop and showroom in a former hospital, a crumbling redbrick building in Hackney. To begin with, though working phenomenally hard, he only made two pairs of shoes a day. Right from the start, he decided to specialise in elegant, handmade evening shoes, which he would sometimes personalise with his initials or other emblems.

In those days I slaved in the workroom all the time. I never went out and I never saw people.

His breakthrough moment came when *Vogue* saw his shoes and made them the subject of an unparalleled 8-page spread in 1988. It was just the publicity he needed to kick-start his couture label. Emma Thompson and Kylie Minogue were two of the first celebrities to place their orders, and more would follow soon.

Jimmy's philosophy has always been that his shoes should be comfortable and practical, as well as looking sensational. If many of his customers came expecting to suffer in the line of beauty, they would be surprised. 'My clients always tell me they

feel transformed each time they slip into my high heels,' he once said. 'Even if some of my high heels look wickedly difficult to wear, they are actually very comfortable.' Jimmy was a perfectionist, and would spend hours fine-tuning the bespoke creations he made for his clients. 'It all has to do with the shape and cut,' he revealed in a rare moment of insight about his increasing success. 'Precision is very important when designing shoes. A good pair of shoes undergoes meticulous technical procedures in order for it to be comfortable for the wearer.' This conscientiousness was one of the reasons his reputation as one of London's finest customised shoemakers steadily grew, mainly by word-of-mouth. 'Beautiful looks mean nothing if the shoes pinch or crush the toes or make a trip from dinner table to loo a chore. Making fabulous-looking shoes is easy. Making them practical to wear is another matter.'

He knew that his clients couldn't fault him for his art, but Jimmy wasn't so confident about his offices. As word about him spread, he started to find London's glitterati queuing up at his door. The basement workshop in a decaying building in an inner-city borough of London was becoming surprisingly popular with society's rich and famous. 'I have to warn them on the telephone that this is not a very nice place,' he told *Footwear News*. An extravagant salon in the West End might have been more to the tastes of his clients, but once they turned up, they weren't worried about the surroundings.

His own appearance was another cause for concern; he didn't exactly feel the part while talking to and fitting his wealthy clients, who included models, actresses and a slew of Sloane girls. 'I used to ask myself whether I look nice enough,' he mused, telling *New Straits Times* that he always felt better when his comb was close to hand – 'I used to have more hair!' he claims. Between his poor English and fears about his appearance, Jimmy was almost painfully shy when he began his business. Now, of course, he is often in the public eye and has got over his awkwardness. 'I learnt to be confident from the British themselves,' he says.

For several years, Jimmy Choo's bespoke shoes were one of London's best-kept secrets. He relied on a highly select, elite group of wealthy clients, who passed his name on to other close friends and those in the business. This, and the self-evident quality of his workmanship, was largely what he relied on for success.

£

CHAPTER 3

Shoes Fit for a Princess

Jimmy's most famous client during these years was undoubtedly Diana, the Princess of Wales.

Diana was one of his most treasured fans, and the client he is 'most proud of'. Keen to revive the British fashion industry, the princess was conscientious enough to only wear clothes and accessories made by British designers. By this stage, Jimmy's star had risen sharply, and his footwear was gracing the catwalks of well-established fashion designers like Giorgio Armani. London's top designers already knew and respected his work. 'So each time Princess Diana visited the studios of Bruce Oldfield, Amanda Wakeley, Jasper Conran, Hardy Amies and Tomas Starzewski,' he said, 'my shoes were piled all over the place. She noticed them, tried them on and luckily, liked them. She had already read about me in the press and asked to meet me through Rachel, an aide to Tomas Starzewski.' It would be the beginning of a long and genuine friendship.

Jimmy was absolutely terrified when Diana asked him to come to Kensington Palace in the summer of 1990. 'I was completely nervous and could not sleep all night,' he remembers. 'I rang my parents and siblings in Penang. I worried over what to wear, what to say and what to do.' Fortunately, the princess was quick to put him at his ease when they eventually met in her apartment at the palace. 'She was very kind and we had afternoon tea together,' he recalls. 'I brought along some samples and drew some sketches for her. She offered me biscuits and I can't remember whether I ate any or not – I was so nervous and shy! But we got on very well.'

She was very, very beautiful, even lovelier in real life than in pictures. Very tall, I think she must have been 5ft 10in, and very stylish.'

I had made her a pair of gold pumps, which she ordered shortly before the accident. I was going to deliver them on Monday but the news came on Sunday. It was very sad. I have kept them in memory of her.

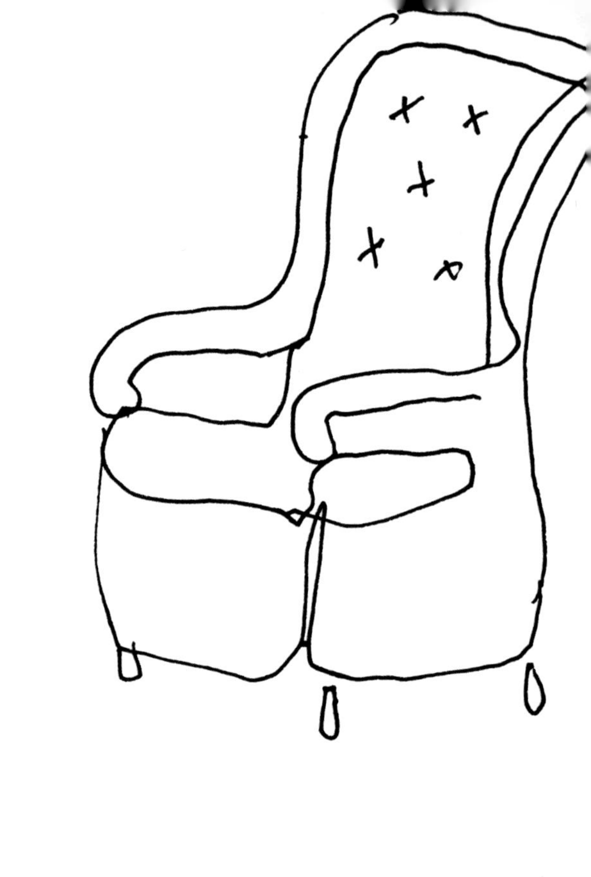

Still, he was daunted at the magnitude of the task she unveiled. 'I was shocked when she showed me her wardrobe and pointed out the dresses that needed matching shoes. I showed her the colour charts and fabric samples and as we collaborated, I became less tense and started to relax. She was size six and a half, UK size, and ordered six pairs on my first visit.'

Over the seven years of their friendship before her cataclysmic death in 1997, Jimmy would lose count of the number of shoes he made for Diana. He was undoubtedly her favourite designer, and she would often call him at his office when she needed a pair of shoes to match a new outfit. The two of them would sit together on the floor and make choices about the shapes, colours and materials to use. Diana would frequently order the same style in several colours, to go with different outfits. When he left, she would help him to repack his cases of samples.

'The princess was a great person and a great friend. She cared about others more than she did about herself,' Jimmy recalled. 'For day wear, she favoured his mid-height pumps, 'but when she wore heels she never wore ankle straps – she wore sling-backs,' he said. However, as she disparagingly told Jimmy, since her husband was significantly shorter than her, she could not wear high heels when she was with him in public.

I feel very much for her two young princes. I can still recall Prince Harry greeting me as the 'kung fu man' whenever I visited Kensington Palace.

After the separation in 1992 and eventual divorce, that began to change. Diana was always one to express herself in her appearance, and Jimmy remembers the change in her clothes and accessories in the years following her break from Charles.

Alongside her rising hemlines, he was asked to make increasingly high heels. 'First she went to 2in, then 3in, then 3½in, then 3¾in. They kept creeping up and up,' he told *The People* in 1998, shortly after her death in Paris.

Diana is not the only member of the Royal Family he has shod. The Duchess of Kent is a regular customer, as is the Duchess of York – like Diana, a fan of sling-back stilettos. Jimmy has never had the honour of making shoes for the Queen, though is of the opinion that a low heel would suit her best: 'probably just about two inches.'

There is no question that Diana's love of Jimmy's work helped to launch his career. His client list steadily expanded, and he found himself working longer and longer hours to keep up with demand. Many would have exploited the opportunities that his reputation brought with it, but the truth was that there was barely time to enjoy himself. He earned a reputation for being a hard worker, and often stayed in his workshop all night, only leaving at 6 am. On one famous occasion, he spent three days and nights non-stop preparing a collection for a Katharine Hamnett show.

Amongst many other honours, one of his commissions involved designing shoes for the James Bond film, *GoldenEye*. Famke Janssen, the Dutch model-turned-actress who played the deadly Xenia Onatopp, is a size 11, which required custom-made heels.

'To survive here you need to do a lot of different styles to catch people's attention,' he maintained. Jimmy found that he constantly had to come up with new ideas to keep his customers interested. Each pair would typically take 2-3 weeks to make, and would cost £200-£500 – significantly cheaper, and faster, than the competition, despite the fact that it was all done by hand. 'I had to aim for this market,' he said, 'because women would not pay these prices for ready-to-wear shoes. The British market for designer shoes is not that large. Also, I want to maintain control. I do not want to pass my designs on to another manufacturer.'

Just occasionally, the pressure would get to him. 'Sometimes in fashion people get angry if you misunderstand what they want: I get angry very fast, but just for ten minutes then it's over,' he told the *Independent on Sunday*. To calm himself and get away from the busyness of everyday life, he liked to go for walks in London parks and feed the birds. Despite his growing fame, his tastes remained inexpensive and he stayed a man of simple pleasures.

I get inspiration for my designs from my own surroundings: in nature, plant, flowers, and sometimes in the interior décor of places that I visit.

When he buys a house he always wants to know if it's the right number house or if the feng shui is correct.

A devout Buddhist, Jimmy is also a firm believer in feng shui, and liked to keep his working environment just so. 'Another thing I believe in is that you need to respect the surroundings,' he said. 'Hygiene is important too. Toilets must be spotless. I'd clean them myself if need be. I'd tell my staff to always keep their hands clean. Then things will turn out good. It is basic feng shui.' John Rocha, a close friend and partner of Jimmy's, remembers. 'When he buys a house he always wants to know if it's the right number house or if the feng shui is correct.'

Jimmy was a victim of his own success. His business was restricted by the number of shoes it was physically possible to make. Even with his trademark long hours, it was getting harder and harder to satisfy his clients' deadlines. 'I've become an iron man,' he told *The Independent* in 1996. His work was taking over his entire life. 'For the last two years I've designed shoes for the band, M People,' Jimmy gave as an example. 'They've offered me tickets to their shows, but I've never had time to go.'

It seemed that Jimmy had gone as far as he could on his own. His shoes were all over the fashion press, top fashion designers asked him to match their collections, supermodels and leading actresses vied for his services, as did sundry British, Jordanian and Malaysian royals. There was undoubtedly a huge demand for his unique designs, but he could only make so many shoes!

VOGUE

CHAPTER 4

In Vogue

At around the same time, an accessories editor for *UK Vogue* was working on a plan to make his creations available to millions. Tamara Yeardye, daughter of the Vidal-Sassoon co-founder Tommy Yeardye and the former Chanel model Ann Davis, had spotted a gap in the fashion shoe market. Tamara had been instilled with a love of fashion, especially shoes, by her mother from an early age.

After spending a short time at *Mirabella* before the magazine folded, she moved to *Vogue* in 1990. In her years of working for the magazine, she realised what a lack of variety there was in the accessories market: here was a huge untapped potential. It was also during this time that she got to know Jimmy's superb work.

'I couldn't find the kind of shoes I wanted to shoot or wear,' she told the *Sunday Mail*. 'Someone told me about Jimmy Choo, this guy who had a few private clients including Princess Diana, and I'd get him to make things up for me in return for a credit.' After they fell out, one of Jimmy's dry asides about Tamara was: 'She boasts about having 500 pairs of my shoes. She never says how many she paid for.'

As Jimmy's star rose, she realised there was a whole lot more potential in expanding his operation. 'His name started becoming known, and I thought "hang on, this is a great platform on which to start a company".'

My dream was for a global luxury brand, younger and funkier than Manolo Blahnik.

She decided to pitch the idea of a ready-to-wear company to Jimmy. A well-known It-girl – her classmates included Tara Palmer-Tomkinson – it had long been Tamara's ambition to start her own accessories business. 'I'd wanted to have my own company since I was young. My dad was a self-made man, and he motivated me. I had a T-shirt business at 17, and opened a stall on London's Portobello Road where I sold my own clothes. He thought that was very enterprising,' she recalled. She had good reasons to focus on footwear: Tamara was a dyed-in-the-wool shoe fetishist. Her favourite song as a child was Nancy Sinatra's 1966 hit 'These Boots are made for Walking'.

'When I was 4 years old, I went on a trip with my convent school to Paris,' she told the *New York Minute*. 'And I begged the nuns to buy me some cowboy shoes I saw in a window. They were terrified of my parents, so I convinced them.'

In addition, her father had made sure she grew up with a keen sense of the value of money. 'I know I had a privileged childhood,' she admitted, 'but I didn't get anything on a plate. He'd do things like match the money I earned on a summer job, but if I didn't earn anything I'd get nothing from him. His mantra was, "Don't overspend." If I do go shopping I have terrible post-purchase guilt. I'd have it if I bought a pair of my own shoes. Which is ironic, right?'

Jimmy Choo once said: 'My wife's shoe closet looks like a boutique; I would look at all those shoes and think to myself that this would be a good business to get into.'

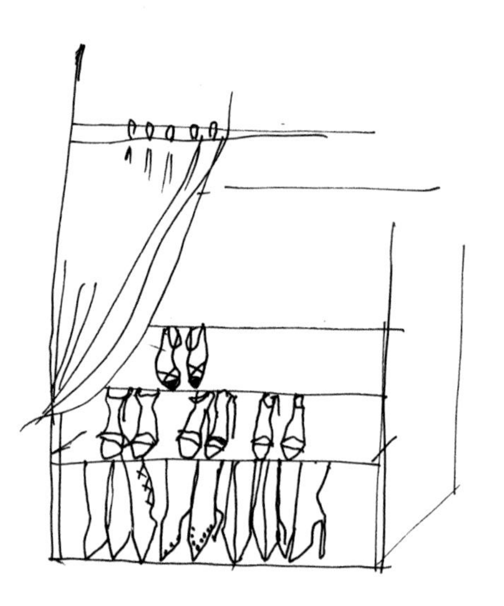

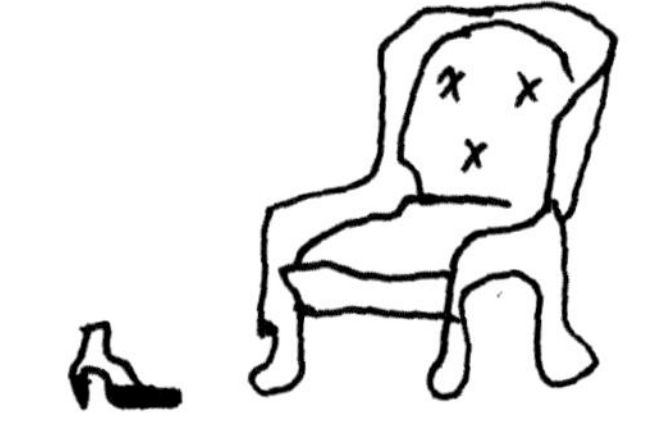

In an industry where the top designers tend to be male, she had an edge. 'Most shoe designers are men, but I know what it feels like to walk around on a four-inch pin,' she said. Her father, who stumped up the money to buy into Jimmy's business, also saw the domestic potential. Neither of them would be disappointed.

In terms of ready-to-wear shoes, Manolo Blahnik was the only real competition for her proposed company. 'That was it,' Tamara said. 'Jimmy was making two pairs of shoes a day, by hand, from a workshop in the East End. My idea was to take the company to a completely different level.' Jimmy was initially reluctant, wanting to make sure he knew his target audience before taking such a risk. Eventually, he realised that the Yeardye money could do for him what even the publicity brought by Princess Diana's custom had not managed to achieve. 'We've taken our time,' he said, 'but after eight years of building up a relationship with clients, I'm confident I know my customer.' Tamara managed to persuade him to part with a 50% share of his company for the sum of £150,000, which she borrowed from her father. It would prove an extremely lucrative investment.

Following her father's death in April 2004, the press would have a field day with his obituaries, in which they thoroughly aired the rumours about Tommy's gangster connections and the ultimate origins of the fortune he had built on his fashion empire. According to the *Evening Standard*, he was a huge bruiser of a man with 'fists like bricks'. Trained as a boxer, he was said to be neither averse nor reluctant to use them to secure his business interests. Back in the 50s and 60s, Tommy could be seen in Winston's, a nightclub favoured by the Kray twins and such-like. His turbulent relationship with Diana Dors, 'Britain's Marilyn Monroe', brought him into the limelight, especially as he sold lurid exposés about her in the national press.

Tamara denies the allegations of violence and financial misconduct, and gangland figures disagree about the extent of Tommy's involvement in their world. What is clear is his ambition to better himself, a characteristic he passed on to his daughter, along with his determination and keen business acumen.

From the beginning, Jimmy was supposed to design the collection, leaving Tamara to take care of the practicalities of sourcing factories and opening stores. 'But we realised early on that there's a big difference between making a pair of shoes and designing a full collection,' she said. 'You have to predict trends. You have to sketch probably over 100 shoes.' Meanwhile, Jimmy was continuing with his couture list, as at this stage it was all he had to pay his wages. It became increasingly clear that his real talent lay in making shoes – not in designing whole collections. At heart he is an artist not a businessman.

on the other side of the lens
Victoria Abril Jonas Akerland Howie B
Emmanuelle Béart Jonas Bjorkman
Elodie Bouchez Patrick Bruel Bill Bryson
Darcey Bussell Eric Cantona The Cardigans
Amira Casar Thomas Castaignède
Roberto Cavalli Eagle-Eye Cherry Jimmy Choo
Helena Christensen Paulo Coelho Ashley Cole
Roman Coppola Sofia Coppola David Coulthard
Douglas Coupland Patrick Cox Alessandro Del Piero
Alain Ducasse Nick Faldo Anni Friesinger
Benno Furmann William Gibson Jefferson Hack
Renny Harlin Joanne Harris PJ Harvey
Tony Hawk Tommy Hilfiger Damien Hirst
The Hives Nick Hornby Natalie Imbruglia
Angelina Jolie Jette Joop Valerie Kaprisky
Adriana Karembeu Jodie Kidd Nicole
Heidi Klum Karl Lagerfeld Henrik
James Lavelle Ron
Russell Mael/Sparks
Carlo

That left Tamara with a problem. She had sunk a large amount of her father's cash into the enterprise, and as yet had little to show for it in the way of designs. It the face of increasing tension, she brought Sandra Choi – Jimmy's niece – on board as Creative Director.

Sandra had been a part of Jimmy's small team of staff since she was a teenager. She had been born on the Isle of Wight, where her father (Jimmy's brother-in-law) owned a Chinese food restaurant. However, not long after she was born, her parents took her back to Hong Kong to be raised by her grandparents. Thirteen years later, the rebellious teenager was getting too much for them. 'She grew into an Adidas-obsessed teenager who shaved the sides of her head and skipped school,' wrote Phoebe Eaton in the *New York Times Magazine*. 'There was make-up, there were Dr. Martens and there were boys. She had started to smoke and was "experimenting with things".' Her grandparents sent her back to the Isle of Wight. After four years in a convent school, she ran away to London to live with her uncle.

Sandra was to become Jimmy's protégée. She began helping him out with his business, making appointments with clients and handling journalists, as well as putting shoes together in the workshop. After finishing school, she applied to St Martin's College to study fashion design. Alongside her course, she maintained her commitments as Jimmy's atelier – an increasingly difficult balance. After only a year, it became clear that she was going to have to make a choice.

One of Sandra's tutors had already pointed out to her that, although she had intended to study fashion, her real talent lay in product development. The couture business seemed to satisfy both interests, and in 1992 she left St Martin's and went to work full time for her uncle – a decision she has never regretted. For some three years before Jimmy Choo expanded into ready-to-wear, Sandra had already been the chief designer and manager of the business. With her experience of the couture business, when Tamara came on board with her irrefuseable offer, she was well placed to step up to the challenge and take on the creative responsibilities. Better still, she immediately saw eye-to-eye with her new managing director and the two formed a strong working partnership. 'She is the architect, and I am the interior designer,' said Tamara. 'She sits down and sketches the structure of the shoe, the bones of it. And then I'll come in, and we'll say: Right. I think that shoe should be in red, kid.' Between them, they would raise Jimmy Choo from a tiny couture outfit into a multi-million pound international phenomenon.

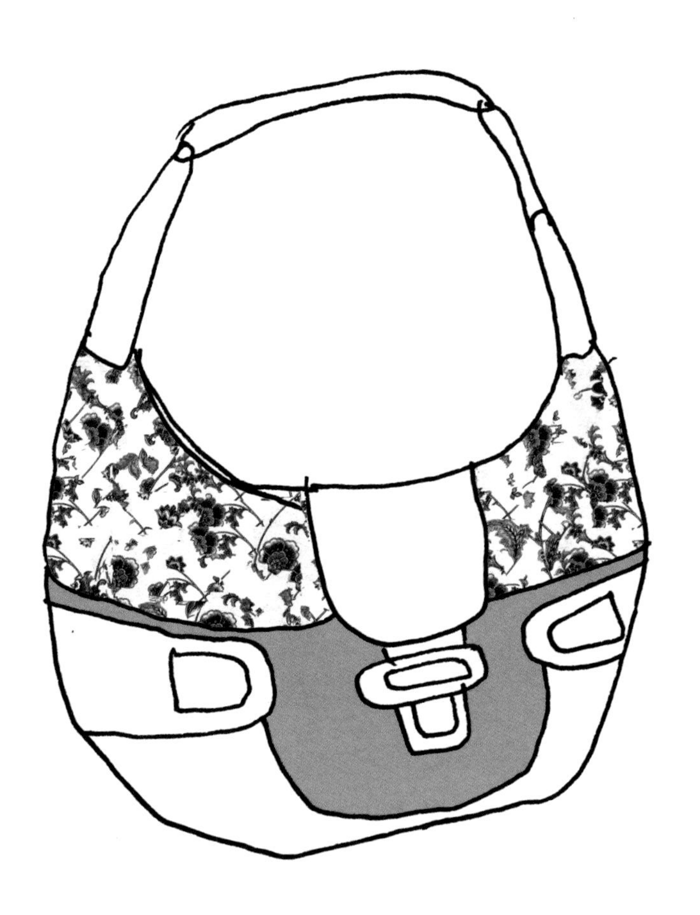

CHAPTER 5

Stepping out

Tamara had not reckoned with the practicalities of starting a new business 'If I knew all the challenges I was going to face I probably would have been too scared to do it,' she told the *Daily Mail* in 2001. 'Sandra and I had an office half the size of this one in a basement below the shop. It had no windows and we worked past midnight every night. We did everything – cleaned the shop, served the customers, designed the collections, did the shipping, produced the orders. We sweated down there.'

Getting the first collection off the ground was hard enough in its own right. Jimmy's studio obviously had neither the space nor the staff to produce the number of pairs they would be selling. As Choi put it, 'To make shoes in England is not easy. We are isolated from components. There are no beautiful heels. There are no beautiful lasts. There is no beautiful leather. It's all in Italy.' Italy, then, was the obvious choice, in terms of expertise and components, but Jimmy's work was unknown there. 'We had no track record,' Tamara complained. 'We just went out there with a few sketches. Being young and women they just wouldn't take us seriously.'

Tamara eventually secured factories to manufacture their first run, opening an office in Italy to deal with shipping and quality control. She also leased a boutique in Knightsbridge – a far cry from Jimmy's previous surroundings. The collection, which retailed from around £100-£300, was designed almost entirely by Sandra

Choi. Tamara had high hopes for her new company, at home and abroad. 'We intend to start slowly, keeping the distribution quite exclusive to start with,' she told *Footwear News* back in 1996. Confident of the attraction to the UK market, she also hoped to export to high-end department stores in the US and Japan.

The first boutique was an instant success, and Tamara immediately began expanding the business. Over the next five years, she opened another three independent boutiques, and their shoes would be sold in another 250 stores across the world. Publicity was helped immeasurably by her relationship with Matthew Mellon II, the son of an extremely wealthy American family that had made a fortune in Gulf Oil and banking.

Tamara described her Jimmy Choo line as: 'They're sexy, but the right side of sexy. They're not tarty. They're comfortable, they're well designed and they've got a sense of fun.'

JIMMY CHOO
JIMMY CHOO
LONDON
JIMMY CHOO
LONDON
JIMMY CHOO
LONDON

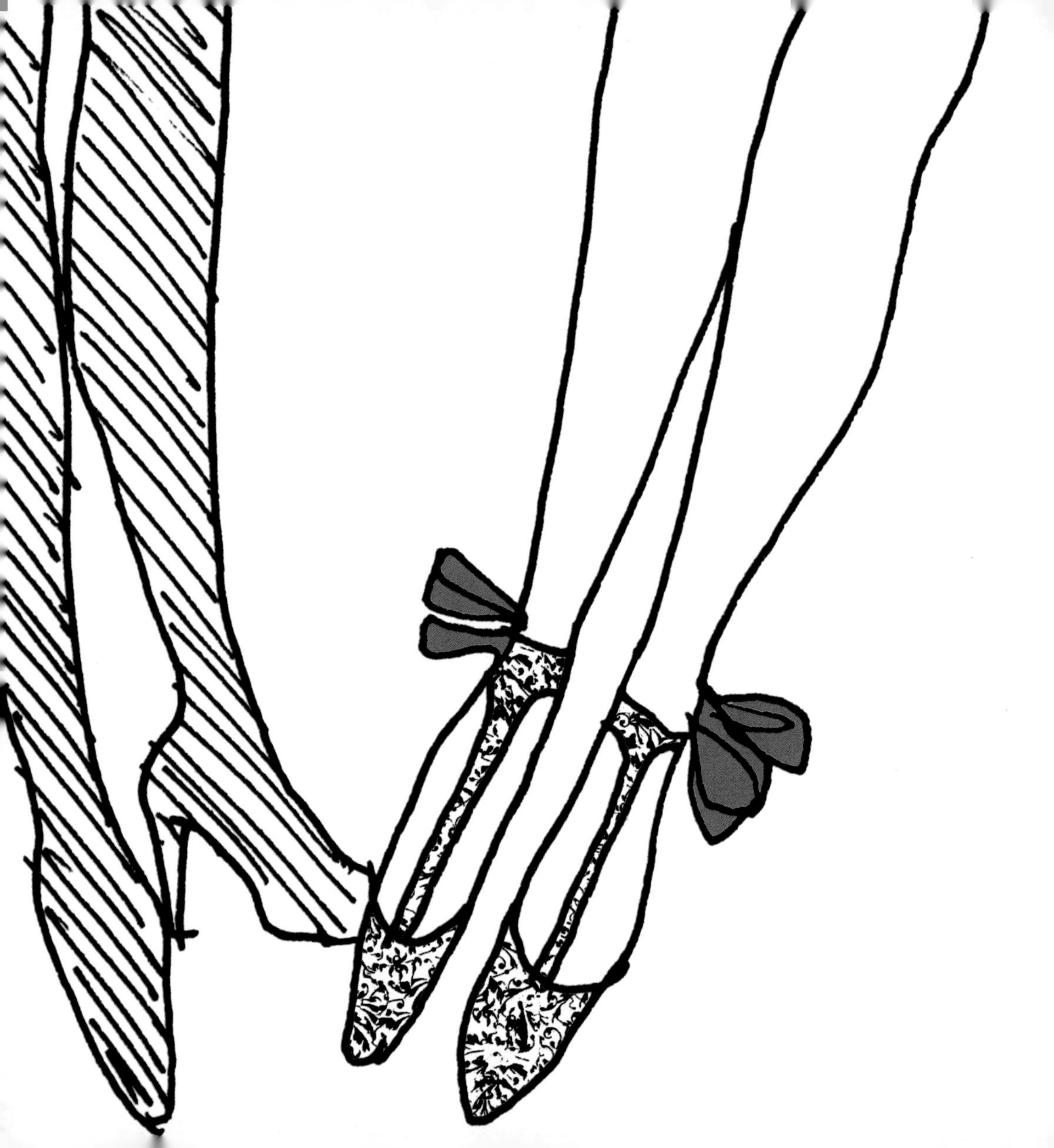

CHAPTER 6

A Piece of the Action

We actually didn't like each other at first,' said Tamara, who first met her husband back in 1996 through Henry Dent-Brocklehurst, a close friend of Elizabeth Hurley. 'We met at dinner with Henry, and then I didn't see him for two years,' she told the *Daily Mail*. 'He said I was an ice queen – which I'm not – and I just thought he was a bit strange. He's quite eccentric and very witty, but he's also very blunt, which English people can find quite shocking.'

Two years later, when they crossed paths for a second time at Henry's wedding in May 1998, she had obviously softened slightly. 'I found him really amusing,' she said. He had changed his opinion of her, too: within four months he had sold his LA house and moved to London to live with her. Matthew, who is also famous for writing speeches for Rudy Giuliani, former New York Mayor, was a venture capitalist. 'He manages his own portfolio and can do it from anywhere with a laptop, so he'll come with me on trips,' said Tamara. In December that year he proposed to her in the course of a helicopter ride over Philadelphia.

Matthew's past may have been cause for some concern. On his 21st birthday, he inherited the sum of $25 million – the first of 13 trust funds to mature. The money was a mixed blessing for someone with indulgent tendencies. Matthew's childhood had not been happy: his parents separated when he was young, and his father was a manic-depressive who committed suicide. Matthew himself nearly died at the age of eleven from alcohol poisoning. In later years, he would broaden his horizons to include cocaine – a habit that also nearly killed him. Throughout his childhood, his mother told him that he would inherit nothing, her intention apparently being to prevent him becoming spoiled. When he got the money after all, it went straight to his head. He bought houses and expensive cars, and spent a lot of time and money partying. 'Heidi Fleiss and the girls used to swing by,' he admits. There were a lot of women, and a lot of coke.

When he got together with Tamara, however, Matthew had been clean for years. Tamara, whose youthful vices had also included alcohol and cocaine ('I was a binger…'), had kicked the habit herself a few years earlier. Beloved of the paparazzi, their romance would propel Tamara – and therefore the Jimmy Choo brand name – into a new era. And Tamara was smart enough to capitalise on the advantage.

Her new fame would enable her to forge connections with Hollywood, and before long, Sandra Choi's strappy, feminine stilettos would be seen on the feet of roll call of *celebettes* sashaying up the red carpet. Moreover, Tamara's own glamorously-clothed, Atkins-slimmed body and model looks made her an ideal showcase, and she tirelessly promoted their creations around the party circuit.

It was an extremely smart move that was to pave the way for Jimmy Choo to contend with the biggest of all their competito – Manolo Blahnik. It was a marketing stategy that completely upstaged Blahnik.

Jimmy Choo had always been a thorn in Blahnik's side as he more-or-less had a captive market until Jimmy's cottage industry made its mark. In the early days, the giant had simply dismissed this minor irritation; now, with Tamara's expansion, the irritation became major.

According to one source close to him, what particularly annoyed him when the Sandra and Tamara's first collections were exhibited was his belief that they had plaigarised some elements of his own designs in their shoes. Given the limited number of variables in shoe design, such accusations are common in the business.

'This is an industry full of knock-offs and slight variations of ideas, and it is impossible to trace who actually had the idea first,' claimed the editor, Michael Atmore, of the much acclaimed *Footwear News*. Blahnik is so obsessed with the belief that other designers lift his ideas that he covers his store windows with a layer of fine mesh to prevent photographs. In the stilletto-stomping world of couture footware, Manolo is renowned for his paranoia about intellectual property rights.

All too aware of the rivalry, Tamara is swift to counter such suggestions, which are made all too frequently. 'I think it is quite insulting because we very much do our own thing,' she told the *New York Times Magazine*. 'Our styles are very different.' Choi, in fact, does occasionally study Blahnik's ideas – not for inspiration, but so that she can go out of her way to design something totally different. Asked once to explain the difference in shape between her own design and Blahnik's, she contrasted her "slicker" heels with Blahnik's "curly whirly…you know: toilet shaped".' There is no love lost here.

By this stage, Jimmy Choo himself had little to do with their business. After providing the initial impetus and his name, he had taken a back seat to the running of the company. Nevertheless, he still picked up the coveted Accessories Designer of the Year at the British Fashion Awards in March 2000. The word from insiders was by then relations between Jimmy and Tamara had almost completely broken down, and Tamara schemed to replace him on stage at the ceremony. However, Jimmy had taken the step of employing his own publicist and lawyer to argue the case for him: but it was now clear that things could not continue as they were for much longer.

Whatever the state of their failing partnership, only two months later Tamara managed to capture the limelight in spectacular fashion when she married Matthew in an extravagant ceremony held at Blenheim Palace. As befits a former *Vogue* editor, Vidal Sassoon heiress and shoe queen, everything was styled to perfection. She wore a $55,000 couture Valentino dress, with a $5 million diamond borrowed from Harry Winston, 'Jeweller to the Stars'. The thrash included a 5-foot wedding cake, 50 white doves, and 30 tables of celebrity guests. Hugh Grant and Liz Hurley were there – seen together for the first time since their split a week earlier – along with Tamara Beckwith, Henry Dent-Brocklehurst, Emma Parker-Bowles and various rentacrowd nobility.

It was a white-tie affair; as the new Mrs Mellon said, 'We all go to so many black-tie events that there's nothing special about it for a wedding.' Besides, she had her image to think about. 'I really wanted men in tails. I think it looks much more glamorous in photographs.' The whole thing was reported to have cost $1 million – though, with a fortune like Matthew's and a company recently valued at $50 million, Tamara barely needed to blink at the expense.

Hello! is said to have offered $150,000 for exclusive coverage of the event, a bid Tamara turned down in favour of *Tatler* and, of course, *Vogue* – the American edition of which devoted no less than 20 pages to the wedding. After the party, the couple left for a 3-week honeymoon in Bali.

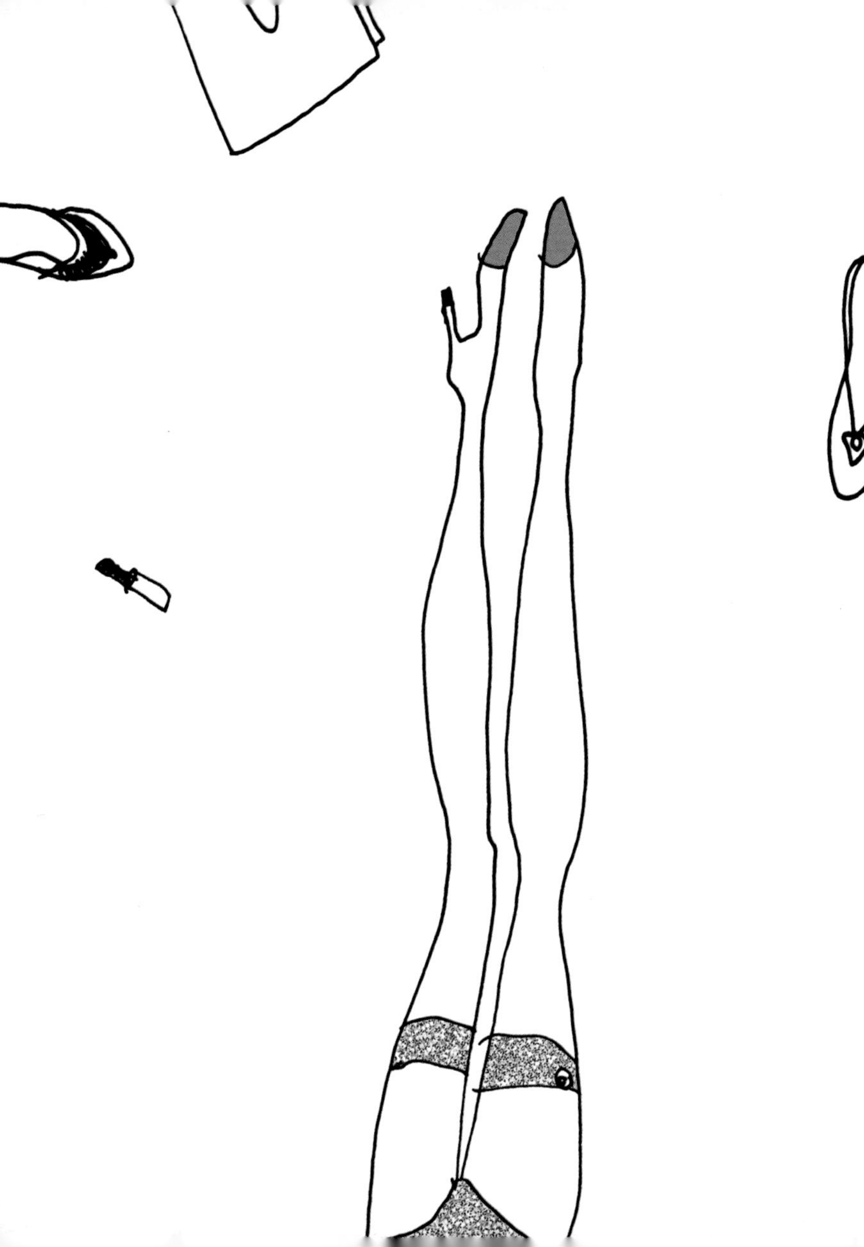

CHAPTER 7

Lost Soles

The next year, 2001, was to see even bigger changes for Jimmy, Tamara and the business. Relations between them were now strained to breaking point. Jimmy's role in the company had receded into the background: Tamara was unquestionably the driving force, and Sandra was responsible for creating the new designs. Despite the fact that Jimmy Choo had been built on his name, Mr Jimmy Choo himself had next to nothing to do with it. Instead, he concentrated his efforts on making shoes for a highly select list of couture clients. In other than the name of the company run by Tamara, they were history.

The split became official in November 2001 with the announcement of a new partnership. Tamara brokered a deal with Equinox Luxury Holdings, a new fashion branch of London-based private equity fund manager Phoenix Equity Partners. The head of Equinox was Robert Bensoussan, previously president of Christian Lacroix. 'I was looking for a company with a very good image and development potential,' Bensoussan said. 'The company is growing at a pace where it's practically doubling its business every year and the business in America remains good.'

Jimmy Choo fit the bill perfectly. Bensoussan stepped in as CEO and Tamara assumed the role of president, knowing that the deal would give their expansion a real boost. But where, exactly, did this leave Mr Jimmy Choo himself?

The fact was that, despite his 50% share, Jimmy had had little to do with the business for a long time. It was a source of great frustration to all involved, and he was as pleased to get out as Tamara was to see him go. When asked about this, the official party line was more diplomatic: Jimmy wanted to concentrate on his bespoke business. 'I am delighted at these new developments – Equinox's involvement allows me to concentrate on the couture aspect of the business and will also allow me more time to pursue educational and other charitable activities,' he told *The Independent* in November 2001. 'Jimmy Choo has always been about couture,' his press officer underlined. 'He wanted to focus on what he likes best.'

Whether or not his fall-out with Tamara and Sandra was the ultimate reason, the deal was considerably sweetened by the deal Bensoussan brokered: Jimmy walked away £21 million better off.

Since then, Jimmy has gone back to doing what he always did best: making bespoke shoes for an incredibly select list of clients. However, his involvement with the company meant things were a little more complicated than that. In fact, adding insult to injury, he actually had to license his own name from Tamara's company to use for his couture business. If that was the ultimate ignominy, he hid it well. Jimmy has always been a good-natured, well-mannered man: he never bleated in public.

I don't work on Sundays and I try to leave the office at 6pm. I like shoes, but I know now there are other things...like people!'

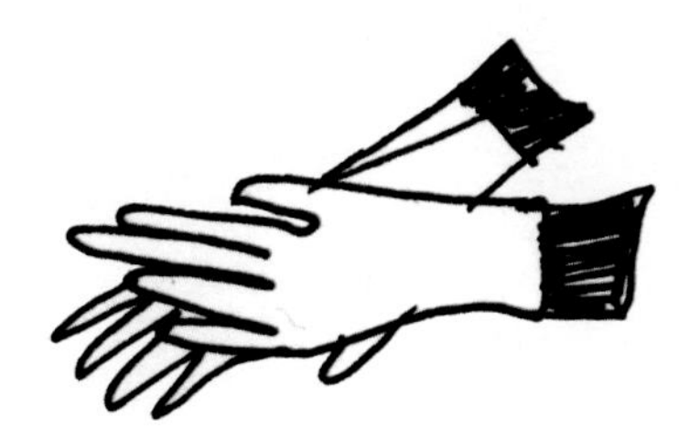

When asked if he minded the fact that he had nothing to do with the company to which he bore his name, he graciously replied, 'No. I respect them and I like what they do.' The deal also gave him more time to spend with his wife, Rebecca – who he met at Cordwainer's and who now works with him in his couture business – and his daughter, Emily. 'I used to just work, but now I have found more time,' he said with relief. Leaving Tamara certainly raised his quality of life.

Doing her best to play down any harmful rumours of unpleasantness between them ('he was very happy to sell out for the amount he got,' she told *The Telegraph* in 2005, when she hadn't so much as spoken to him in four years), Tamara pushed the new incarnation of the company forwards. With Equinox's money behind her, there were plans to open another 20 stores in the next five years. With Bensoussan's cash, her media appeal and Sandra's design talent, the future of Jimmy Choo was looking extremely corporate. Unfortunately for her, the same could not be said for Tamara's personal life.

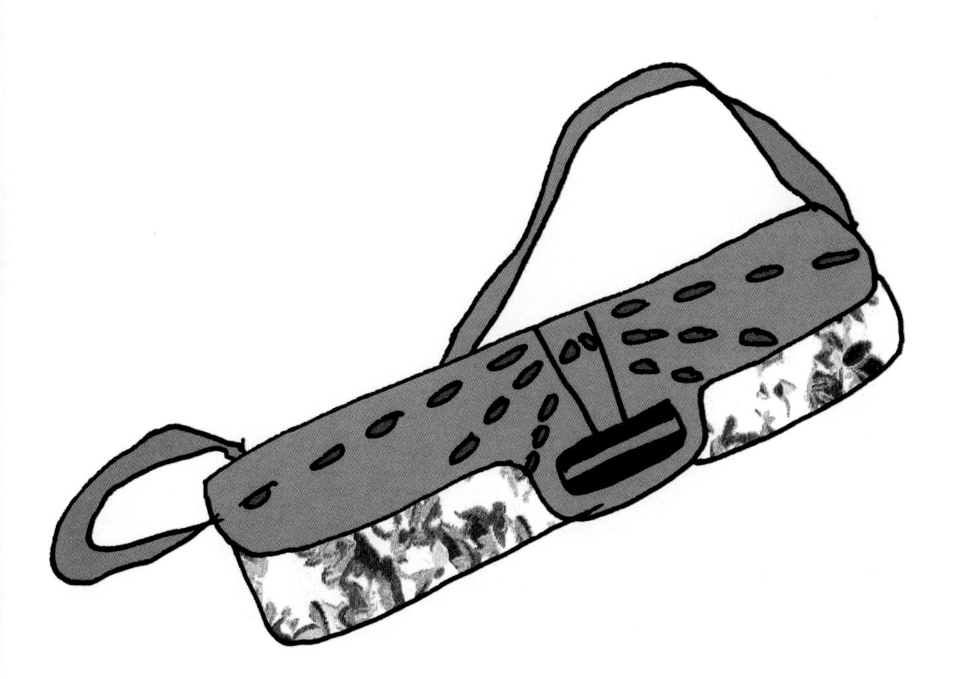

JimmyShoe

Jimmy

CHAPTER 8

Coo-coo, ca-Choo, Mrs Robinson?

For a while, Tamara seemed to have it all. Women were going wild for her 'Jimmy Choos' – it was a mark of the measure of her success that the name had become rhyming-slang for a pair of sophisticated, sassy evening shoes – she had a celebrity lifestyle, new marriage and, by 2002, a young daughter, Araminta 'Minty' Mellon.

In August of 2003, with Jimmy Choo expanding into Europe and Asia, as well as record sales in the US and UK, the Mellons took a much-needed holiday with a group of friends in Ibiza. It was to prove Matthew's undoing. 'I had some concerns about my business, and there were already some stresses on my relationship with Tamara,' he later said. 'We both travel constantly and it puts a stress on any relationship. I didn't adapt well to being on a party island in the midst of these other pressures.'

Sober for years, while out partying on night he bumped into one of his old dealers. The predictable happened. Some months later, fresh out of rehab and in full confessional mode, he told all to the *Evening Standard* : 'In every city and country in the world where I travel, I have a Fixer, either a man or woman, who organises everything for me and can get me anything I want. My Fixer was there and I wanted cocaine. I asked her – it wasn't as if she was pushing it.' So began a 48-hour drug binge that would throw his life back into disarray and pave the way for one of the most unlikely celebrity affairs.

'Matthew would say he'd be off for an hour and he'd come back two days later,' Tamara confided to the *Daily Mail.* With her husband acting increasingly erratically, Tamara had few sources of support. Oscar Humphries was one of them.

Oscar was the 22-year-old son of Barry Humphries, the brilliant Australian creator of Dame Edna Everage. He and Tamara had been introduced by mutual friends, and he had joined the family on their ill-fated Ibiza holiday. Oscar himself was well-known for his coke-fuelled antics, which include hotel-room trashing and a suicide attempt after a very public dumping by society girl Octavia Khashoggi. A few weeks after the holiday, with Matthew still drifting in and out of her life in a haze of booze and drugs, Oscar and Tamara – as she was 13 years older than him he dutifully became her toyboy – struck up a strong friendship. What happened next was published in all its bizarre detail in *The Telegraph*, using poorly-concealed identities that provoked immediate (and correct) speculation.

'When, weeks later, she cornered me in a bar, looked me in the eyes and said, simply: "I really, really like you and I want you to come home with me", I was paralysed with fear and insecurity,' Oscar wrote, in an article signally reminiscent of Benjamin Braddock's encounter with Mrs Robinson."Why me?" I thought. "This woman clearly needs a man, but I'm just a boy." Now, of course, I realise that she didn't need anything or anyone. But she knew what she wanted – and how to get it.'

'It felt like I had about five seconds to make up my mind. "Should I go through with this?" I asked myself. "Is this something I really want?" And then I remembered having watched *The Graduate* when I was 15 (and still a virgin), and thinking "Why don't things like that ever happen to me?" And I remembered reading Colette's *Cheri* and thinking how sexy it all was. And now at 22, it actually was happening to me. What could I do? I took the plunge and was led to her bedroom. I felt completely powerless. She, after all, had made this happen. I felt like I had no say in what was taking place.' Of course, Oscar could also feel a scoop – all right, lucrative – article writing itself. How could he resist?

Oscar claimed he never intended to unmask his older lover to the world: in his article, he claimed that she was a 40-year-old divorcée, rather than the married, 35-year-old multimillionaire president of an international company. Nevertheless, it didn't take a Sherlock Holmes to figure out the truth. The ardent affair between Oscar and Tamara soon became public knowledge, and would place even more pressure on her strained marriage with Matthew – who, for his part, had taken up with Russian millionairess Katia Moulari, though she somehow did not merit such intense coverage as Tamara's paramour.

Tamara's vulgarity made Mr Jimmy Choo cringe... and Mr Jimmy Choo was how he now known. Given that Equinox owned the intellectual property rights to his name, he has to use something to differentiate him from the company. Aside from all that cash, there had been a little compensatory bonus in the form of OBE, in June 2003, for his contribution to shoe design and in making London the design centre of the world. Even with honours up for bids, it is doubtful if even the Blair government – well Lord Levy – would have taken Tamara's money.

Needless to say, she and Oscar didn't last long. 'I did have an affair with Oscar but it was just a brief fling that meant nothing,' she finally admitted, after weeks of silence. 'Oscar used me as a vehicle to sensationalise an article at my expense. He's young and impressionable and wants a career as a journalist – I understand that's why he did what he did.' All the same, she claims not to harbour any resentment. 'He was charming, made me laugh and was wonderful company. Everyone seems hooked on the Mrs Robinson thing, but it was more than that. Oscar became a great friend and I'm still very fond of him,' she told the *Daily Mail*. 'Falling for Oscar was something I never expected to happen. But when Matthew was off every day drinking himself into oblivion, Oscar was there.'

CHAPTER 9

Putting the Boot in

She and Matthew tried to patch things up, but between the affairs and the drugs, it was not to be. The couple separated, and he later filed for divorce. Matthew was clearly looking for a fight. Not only did he sue for joint custody of Minty, their 3-year-old daughter, but he also went after a chunk of the Jimmy Choo money. Despite his status as heir to the £4 billion oil and banking fortune, he claimed that the shoe empire had been built on his reputation. 'I was floored by that,' said Tamara. 'People buy the shoes because of his name?' Matthew hired one of the most ferocious divorce lawyers around, Raymond 'Jaws' Tooth, who had represented Sadie Frost against Jude Law, as well as Eric Clapton's ex-wives.

'Sometimes, when you're in the public eye, the spotlight shines into areas you'd prefer to keep private,' Tamara admitted. 'But you've got to ride it out. I think I'm strong enough to do that.' The negative publicity may not have been comfortable, but it only helped Jimmy Choo. Aided by the paparazzi coverage, the expansion spearheaded by Bensoussan saw sales in excess of $40 million by the end of 2003.

Since then, Tamara has been linked with Flavio Briatore, Pharell Williams and rock star Kid Rock, but claims that, after Matthew, marriage is not for her. 'I've found getting divorced to be one of the most painful experiences. I thought marriage was for ever, and it's devastating when it doesn't work out.' The friction between them is still evident: Matthew was recently arrested for tapping her phones and bugging her house, in part of a scandal that also saw NHS computers being hacked into for the purposes of blackmail.

The rocky ride was not yet over for Tamara. Just as her life was beginning to stabilise, she was once more shaken – this time by the death of her father in April, 2004. On a roll from the drugs and toyboy stories of the last year, the tabloids raked up stories about Tommy Yeardye's involvement in the gangland underworld of the 1950s and 60s. Tabloids being tabloids fully appreciate the legal ruling that you cannot libel the dead. Already fragile, this was more than Tamara could handle: she was very close to her father, with whom she spoke every day.

The slur on his memory was particularly painful. 'I am still reeling from the shock of what has been written because it is the complete antithesis of the person I and his many friends knew,' she told the *Evening Standard* after reading their article. 'For me it is like reading about a stranger, just complete and utter lies. Shortly before he died, he finished writing his autobiography. I have been reading through the early chapters to see if there is any mention of him hanging out with the Krays and such gangster types, and there is nothing. I am so upset – he was the absolute anchor of my life.'

At least Matthew had eased up on her. 'In the end Matthew fired Raymond,' she told the *Evening Standard*. 'He said, "You are destroying my relationship with my wife." So we sat down together and worked things out between ourselves.' After her father's death, the rest of her family moved to LA. 'My parents had planned to move anyway so my mother just followed through,' she said. 'I feel pulled in a million different directions. I feel like my life constantly goes at 100 miles per hour and I don't have anybody.' It was a rare moment of weakness for a businesswoman with a reputation as a steely, unrelenting machine, albeit one with despite the thunder thighs a stunning dress sense and, naturally, great heels.

Meanwhile, Jimmy Choo was on the up-and-up. Later that year, US investment firm Hicks Muse bought a 78% stake in a deal that valued the company at £101 million. The executive team of Tamara, Sandra and Bensoussan remained unchanged, and the additional financial backing helped realise their plans to expand into handbags and other accessories. Tamara clarified: 'My vision is to accessorise a woman completely – her sunglasses, her belts, her lingerie, her cosmetics, her swimwear, her perfume.'

Once again, the future was looking very, very Choo.

Accessories are where you get your status now that clothes are so casual.

Tamara Mellon, 2004

CHAPTER 10

The Ones to Wear

Today, with yearly sales in excess of £50 million and plans for 47 freestanding stores by the end of 2006, the phenomenon shows no signs of stopping. From its humble origins as the couture business of a soft-spoken Malaysian cobbler in a Hackney basement, Jimmy Choo has become a worldwide sensation and a by-word for glamour and sophistication.

Far more than his only rival Manolo Blahnik ('My shoes are special shoes for discerning feet'), the Choo brand has turned fashion shoes into a respectable... no, into a desirable fetish. Sarah Jessica Parker's character, Carrie Bradshaw, in *Sex and the City* had an entire episode revolving around how she had spent $40,000 footwear, mainly on Choos, while not being able to afford her own apartment.

In Her Shoes, starring Cameron Diaz, is based on a storyline about two sisters with opposite personalities with their shoe size being the only thing they have in common – the wild child sister, played of course by Diaz, wears a dazzling range of Jimmy Choos. Naturally, the conventional po-faced sister ends up sharing her taste for such decadent footwear.

Shoes are now iconic and, like perfume, overturn the normal laws of economics – to be worthwhile, they have to be expensive. Cheap shoes are like cheap perfume, by definition nasty. Marshal Colhen, chief analyst of the The NPD Group, a influential consumer information company based in Washington DC commented recently on this change: 'Footwear has become a fanatical purchase for even those women who never had a footwear fetish before. Apparel is no longer the highest priority in women's wardrobes: handbags and footwear have become the signature items used to project personal taste, wealth and style.'

The NPD Group point out that the market in fashion footware is now $20 billion worldwide. And 1% of that is for shoes costing $1,000 and up. While the Choo brand does not dominate the market – Manolo, Gucci, Ferragamo are all big – it has driven this cultural and economic change. In the UK shoes still provide some 65% of Jimmy Choo revenue with the rest coming from bags, and small accessories. In other markets the mix is more towards 50-50.

In August 2006, Robert Bensoussan, the chief executive of Jimmy Choo, attended a conference of luxury goods companies held at the Harvard Business School. He told the delegates: 'We don't want Jimmy Choo to be known as a shoe brand.' After the launch of a handbag line in 2003, the company began developing fragrances, eyewear and even jeans: Bensoussan said that the brand extension to push the turnover from a $100m to $200 is being done 'very carefully'. But, nota bene, it is being done.

Meanwhile, Tamara Mellon is as global as the brand that she more than anyone turned into a worldwide phenomenon. In November 2005, she made the cover of *Newsweek* as 'one of the world's most powerful women'. She was quoted: 'I've created a business but, because of the nature of the product, it has glamour attached. I don't look square or suity – people are confused.' Charlize Theron, Gisele Bundchen, Gwen Stefani, Julia Roberts, Penelope Cruz, Keira Knightley, Uma Therman, Rachel Weisz...have all trod into that red Oscar carpet in their Jimmy Choos and Tamara has been on hand to ensure that the merchandise was just right. Her stroke of genius, of course, was to exploit the marketing potential of shodding these 'global reach' stars with Jimmy Choos.

But while she seems to have kicked the cocaine and booze she still has a taste for bad boys who clearly haven't. Her latest is hell-raiser Kid 'Son of Detroit' Rock who has also dated Pamela Anderson and Jaime Pressley. The 6' 5", 35-year-old rap-rocker came out with Tamara when they attended the wedding of Elton John and David Furnish. Kid Rock is heavy dude with a taste for right-wing politics. He is also generous with his time in supporting causes that he believes in. He is loved by the grunts in the marines for the way he gives regular and free concerts for the combat troops. It seems an unlikely union but for now they are supposed to intoxicated with each other.

Vespa

VOGUE

Tamara's tumultuous love life makes it unlikely that she will end up happy-ever-after with Kid Rock. Her recipe for happiness, however, is economic rather than romantic. 'Make your money and buy your freedom,' she extols. 'I would love to inspire women to take responsibility for themselves, to not be dependent on men. Because then you can be truly happy.' Tamara has an estimated £60 million happiness habit, which must mean she is quite ecstatic.

Tamara's flamboyance has also managed to push Sandra Choi to the brink of resigning with her constant boasts that she is the creative force behind the label. Yet, Tamara still dances in the limelight. Last year, 44 stars including 'Cocaine' Kate Moss, Victoria Beckham, the Duchess of York and Tamara Mellon herself posed wearing nothing more than their Jimmy Choos and a few pieces of Cartier jewellery for *4 Inches*, a coffee-table book to raise money for AIDS orphans in Africa.

Whether it saved many orphans is doubtful, but whatever happens to Tamara, Jimmy himself will continue in his craft and until global warming revives going barefoot it is difficult to envisage the brand going out of fashion. Women the world over love the expressive, graceful heels inspired by Jimmy, designed by Sandra Choi and made famous by Tamara Mellon.

If I have any justification for having lived it's simply that I'm nothing but faults, failures and so on, but I have tried to make a good pair of shoes. There's some value in that.

Arthur Miller [playwright, 1915-2005]